What if your mother

What if your mother

Judith Arcana

To Rebecca —
what a joy to find another
colleague — in you — a woman
who thinks & acts about what
we know needs to be thought &
acted about — Judi
3/06

Chicory Blue Press, Inc.

Goshen, Connecticut

Chicory Blue Press, Inc.
Goshen, Connecticut 06756

Printed in the United States of America.

Book Designer: Virginia Anstett
Cover Art: Abigail Marble

Several pieces in this collection appeared first in the following publications, some in different versions and/or with different titles: *Witness; 5AM; 13th Moon; Calyx; Prairie Schooner; Hurricane Alice; Passager; Motherwork; Sojourner; Elixir; Affilia; POOL; poem/memoir/story; Reproductive Health Matters, The Women's Global Network for Reproductive Rights Newsletter;* and *Family Reunion, Poems about Parenting Grown Children* from Chicory Blue Press, 2003. NOTE: "Eggs," "Family Resemblance" (now "Multigravida") and "Maternal Instinct" are reprinted from PRAIRIE SCHOONER, fall 2000, by permission of the University of Nebraska Press. Copyright 2000 by the University of Nebraska Press. "Facts of Life" is reprinted from PRAIRIE SCHOONER, spring 2004, by permission of the University of Nebraska Press. Copyright 2004 by the University of Nebraska Press. "Great With Child" appears in *A Fierce Brightness, twenty-five years of women's poetry* from CALYX PRESS, 2002.

I am grateful to the Doctoral Faculty of the Union Institute, Soapstone, The Montana Artists Refuge, The Mesa Refuge, The Helene Wurlitzer Foundation, The Rockefeller University Archive Center, The Deming Foundation/Money for Women, Literary Arts, and The Puffin Foundation for grants, awards and residencies during the years of this writing. Many thanks to Tom Rosenbaum and Michelle Powers at the Rockefeller Archive Center for their assistance; thanks also to the staff at the Schlesinger Library.

My gratitude to those who read this work in manuscript and talked with me about the poems: Judith Barrington, Peaches Bass, Pat Cason, Ron D'Aloisio, Roberta Dyer, Susan Gidding-Green, Sue Ann Higgens, Bob Nichols, Grace Paley, Minnie Bruce Pratt, Marian Rodriguez, Tareyn Tamez, and my excellent publisher/editor, Sondra Zeidenstein. More thanks: for thrilling art, Abbey Marble; for research assistance, Rebecca Alpert and Claire Smith; for useful conversation, Ruth Gundle, Nancy LaPaglia, Ursula K. LeGuin and Rebecca Shine; for financial assistance, Dick and Fred Rosenfield; for the chapbook version of "She Said," Daniel Arcana and Natalie Frigo; and to Cindy Cooper for adapting "She Said" for the theater in *Words of Choice*. And my love to my dear partner Jonathan, who has supported and encouraged my writing for thirty years.

Library of Congress Cataloging-in-Publication Data
Arcana, Judith.
What if your mother / Judith Arcana.
p. cm.
Includes bibliographical references.
ISBN 1-887344-11-x (pbk.)
1. Mother and child—Poetry. 2. Motherhood—Poetry. 3. Abortion—Poetry.
4. Mothers--Poetry. I. Title.
PS3601.R38W47 2005
811'.54–dc22

2005018114

This work is dedicated to the memory of two women: Annie Solomon Rosenfield, who had an abortion in 1937 and then had my older brother and me in 1939 and 1943; and Gwendolyn Brooks, whose poem "The Mother" was the first one I ever read about abortion.

Table of Contents

Preface xi

Separating argument from fact

Not Really a Baby 3
Eggs 4
Sperm 5
My Father Tells Me Something, 1973 6
What If Your Mother 7
Think Fast 8
Sealed Birth Records Challenged in Court 9
Lucky 10
She Was Only an Embryo 11
For You It Was Another 13
You Don't Know 14
Multigravida 15
Sleeping like a Baby 16
Loverchild 17
Sometimes 18
Snow, Fall 20
Chickens 21
We Know These Things 22

Information rarely offered

Maternal Instinct 25
Carhop, 1956: Her First Job 26
Birth Control 27
She Couldn't Be Sure What He'd Say 29
Lola Dee, Cleveland Street 31
Movie Notes *(incl. actors)* 33
Courage under Fire 36
Patient History 38
The Bible in Everyday Life 39

Don't tell me you didn't know this

Jocasta Interviewed in Hell 43
Talking about Suzie, 1959 44
Sheila's Deposition, 1997 45
Birth Mothers Turn to Highest Court 47
Noreen's Phone Calls, 1999 49
Great with Child 51
That Will Never Happen 52
The Spade 53
Abort/Retry/Fail 54
The Train Is in the Station 56
All These 57
Women 59
For All the Mary Catholics 60
Opposing Arguments 61
Obstetrician Murdered by Terrorist in Amherst, New York 62
Back and Forth 63

Here, in the heart of the country

Woman Finds Truth 67
Facts of Life 68
Hard Times, Fast River 69
Being Alive 70
In the Service We Said 71
City Living, Chicago 72
Applied History 73
Women's Liberation 74
The Teacher at Home, 1970 75
Glenda Charleston, 1971 76
Here Is What Happened. 78
Felony Booking, Women's Lockup, Eleventh & State: A Short Literary Epic 79

Yes and No 82
She Said 83

Notes 89

Preface

Thirty-five years ago, one evening in the fall of 1970, I walked into a small church on West Fullerton Parkway in Chicago to attend an orientation meeting for new members of the Abortion Counseling Service of the Chicago Women's Liberation Union. I was twenty-seven years old and had been wondering for a year or so where to find – how to sign up with – this women's liberation movement I'd been hearing so much about.

Seven years ago, one morning in the spring of 1998, I stood in the kitchen of my house in Northeast Portland, Oregon, breaking eggs – separating whites from yolks for a complicated recipe I had propped up in front of me as I worked. I was fifty-five years old and had been thinking about how to use what I'd learned since 1970 to be more useful in the increasingly frightening national struggle over abortion and motherhood.

Sunlight was streaming through the kitchen windows, hot and bright, making the egg yolks glow and the whites shine clear as mountain water. I thought about how those eggs were like my own, like anybody's eggs. I thought about what eggs *are*. I stared at the eggs; I stopped moving my hands. And then, as if I were starring in a wildly romantic fantasy about poetry and the lightning arrival of the mysterious muse, I dropped the eggs, swiped my hands across a towel, grabbed a pencil and scratch paper and began scribbling fast, to hold onto the words and images suddenly flooding my mind.

When the fit passed, I looked at what I'd written. I put the eggs away, took the scribbles up to my office and began to work on the poem now called "Eggs." It was followed by the poem called "Chickens" (thereby answering that old riddle, I guess) as well as "Maternal Instinct," the poem now called "Multigravida" and the first version of "Yes and No" – and when those five were all in progress, I saw that my work as a poet had rushed, river-like, into a startling confluence with my work as an activist.

Some of this writing was seeded by my pre-Roe abortion work, but most of it is drawn from more recent experience: the lives of women and girls I know or have simply encountered; newspapers, elections, legislation; the terrorism and assassination perpetrated by the stridently successful anti-abortion movement in the USA; work with clinics and the staunchly committed people and organizations who are doing the necessary brave work for reproductive health and abortion rights.

A handful of these poems I wrote a long time ago and recently surprised myself by realizing they belong in this collection, but most I wrote between the spring of 1998 and the fall of 2004, years when I began again – this time as a poet – to work deliberately in the women's liberation movement I went looking for in 1970.

Judith Arcana
Portland, 2005

Separating argument from fact

Not really a baby

Most of us think it's not really a baby,
not a baby at all when it's that small.
We see pictures on a screen, strange
dim images shot back from space.
But we know science isn't what you feel.
What you feel comes from inside,
movement grandma calls *quickening*.
Until then we count on the calendar
to where we'd have to be to have it
be a baby: like if you let it grow
those chubby bumps into fingers,
it would be because of the fingers;
lots of us think it's a baby then,
with legs and arms, even if the eyes
look like they're from another planet.
That's when all the pictures fit inside
your family album; that's when
most of us think it really is a baby.

Eggs

Separating eggs in the kitchen, she is
separating argument from fact, the babies –
all that yelling while the babies are inside;
they're all yolk and sticky, they are eggy babies;
pouring slow yolk from one broken shell to another,
letting the white slip down the sink, saving the yellow
for chocolate cake, banana bread, hollandaise
while their heads are big and glazed,
their eyes are pingpong balls, hands like paddles,
tiny spines like rubber whips: slower than chickens,
slower than cats and dogs; we argue months
while they roll inside their outer space, thickening.

Sperm

In Science class we learned sperm cells carried whips;
flagellates, the teacher said. We pictured medieval
fanatics from History class, who hurt themselves to love
their god. One day the teacher had a thin bright snake
sliding through the belt loops on his khakis. He let us
touch it, saying, *This one looks like a coral snake,*
but he can't hurt you. You can just imagine
what we thought, said, drew in our notebooks.
From cartoons we moved to textbook illustration,
slides on the microscope stage. In college,
still sketching and laughing, we wondered:
Was this truly motile sperm on our slides?
Did they jerk off for our lab kits? So many boys had
offered this – it could be true. (We never smelled semen,
only formaldehyde, plastic chairs and after-shave.)

But there they were, jerky, blind, hesitant little swimmers
with tails of thread. Like tadpoles you catch in a jar,
then wait for the legs to jut muscular angles, to kick
with knobby fingered webbing, to bump up chunky heads,
no necks, like third year football players. But sperm would never
leap right into moonlight shivering in black pond water.
Sperm were frantic as they thrashed across the thin glass slide,
no egg nearby. Finally they dropped their tails, melting
into communion on a movie screen above the chalkboard;
someone had filmed their kamikaze ecstasy to teach us.
They didn't care about being watched. We saw them
whip their tiny bodies toward the beloved egg, pierce
her membrane and then die, mimicking the men
who made them, pumping and thrusting through
their cloud of milt until they get there, release, fall away.

My father tells me something, 1973

You know, your mother had an abortion, it was before you and the boys were born, in the thirties, about a year after we got married, so let's see – we must have been twenty-one, both of us. She went, Annie went, to our family doctor, it was Jack Kornofsky, your mother's cousin – well, he married your mother's cousin Dorothy – he was the one we went to whenever anything was wrong, he would come out to the house when you kids got sick, do you remember him at all? He wore glasses, had a big smile. He would come when you had a fever, and he would always bring a Hershey bar in his bag for you kids – imagine a doctor doing that! He and Dorothy were at our wedding. So anyway, he told your mother she was pregnant. When she came home and told me, we went back to him together, you know, and asked him what we should do. We didn't think about it the way you do, the way everybody does now, we didn't talk about it, we just knew it wouldn't be good if we had a baby then, so young, just starting out. This was the Depression, we were still living with your grandparents in the old house on Saywell. So we asked him, Kornofsky, what to do. He sent us to this other doctor – oh listen, all of a sudden I remember his name, it was Ryan, his name was Ryan, can you beat that? All these years never thinking about it, why should I suddenly remember his name? So Kornofsky gave us the address and phone number of this other doctor, Ryan, who would do abortions. But no, no, if he hadn't told us what to do, who to see, hadn't given us the address, I guess she would have had to have the baby, we wouldn't have known what else to do, I don't know what else there would have been to do. Maybe your mother would have had some other ideas, maybe the women could do something, like you, now – but you know, I don't think so. As I remember it, she didn't know any more than I did.

What if your mother

Sometimes when you talk to them, in argument
they say, What if your mother had an abortion?
And then I say she did, because it's true, only
that one wasn't me, it was somebody else; nobody
but my mother ever knew that baby. But they
mean me, the people who say it, mean
what if she aborted me, like that's hard
to answer. They're so stupid, because what if
she miscarried or gave me away? What if
I drowned at the beach when I was three?
What if she loved someone else, not my dad?
Then I wouldn't be here either. What if, what if.
What's the point of asking this phony question?
All you could ever answer is, Then everything
would be different, wouldn't it? One thing sure,
I wouldn't be standing here talking to some jerk
who asked me that dumb question. I wouldn't
be mad at my mother for doing it – would I?
I think you just have to tell these people,
Get real. That's not what it's all about.

Think Fast

Like a quiz show, clocks are ticking,
the audience is screaming right at you;
there are prizes, there are choices:
if you want to, call it a baby
right from the start but
if you don't, if you can't,
if you just *can't,*
then call it an embryo,
clustered cells dividing, splitting –
(I don't mean they're leaving home:
with one choice they stick around,
getting taller all the time, standing
at your fridge, door wide open,
drinking milk out of the bottle
even though you told them not to) –
you've got to decide right now
if you want it: *can* you have it?
You don't get much time.

Sealed Birth Records Challenged in Court

In the old days, everything was secret:
you went away to what they called a home
or you stayed inside your own, hiding
your belly when you knew you could not
keep it; all the signs were danger signs:
breasts heavy with yellow cream,
darkening nipples, widening hips,
desires for food, sex, sleep all growing
with the child while you stood wide-footed,
moving side to side like a broad-bottomed boat
riding the long tide going out without you;
salty water shifting with a small internal moon
until eclipse, when they took the child away
and you'd never see it, never know its name,
never know if the eyes darkened, mind sharpened,
curious about you – if they talked about you,
if they said you were first, said you held the baby first.

Lucky

First child a boy, sweet little person
starting to talk, wanting to read.
Almost enough money
(hard to get enough money)
to be a good mother.
Then this one starts up:
Surprise! Then uh oh, no daddy.
Ahh, maybe keep it anyway.
This could be a little girl,
dreamy lovermother says;
then she'd have a pair:
Dick and Jane, Jack and Jill,
Hansel and Gretel. But no one
granted her three magic wishes.
She knew what she should do:
decision colored sticky red,
shining like an exit sign,
glowing in the dark
like a stoplight. Lucky
for the little girl, safe
from all the big bad wolves –
all those scary stories
she'd never have to hear –
no bad dreams or screams.

She was only an embryo

Not yet a fetus, only five weeks
not much of a thinker
not smart like her brother
her father or mother
not many IQ points in there.
Not like all those tall relations
she was (maybe) one fifth of an inch.
No arms or hands
she couldn't see
she wasn't much to look at.
No sweet little rosebud lips
attached to what the doctor
(to be honest) called
the primitive mouth cavity
another part as early
as her roundly pointed tail.
She did have something
like a heart
but you couldn't say
(even kindly)
that it was in the right place.

Looking at the one
who would have been
big brother, sleeping
small now, warm and rosy,
Grandma, shocked and sorry, whispered
What did the baby look like?
Then Mama (having looked)
having clearly seen
the contents of the beaker
told the truth (just like the doctor)
I'd say strawberry jam, Ma.

I'd say that baby
looked just like strawberry jam.

For you it was another

For me it was one thing
for you it was another
you the diver under water
living like a fish, baby
gills and fins soon melting
down into a thickening pool of cells
shoulders growing wide out of your back
fingers and thumbs on two hands at the ends
of arms that might have been raised years later
on the high board, your body's arrow shape
reminding us of where we come from
when you leap to cut the surface
slip into deep water, disappear

You don't know

You think I didn't care about that baby,
didn't wonder if we'd like each other
when she turned fourteen;
didn't think he'd follow anywhere
his older brother went.
You think we take them out, like gangsters;
disappear them, like generals.
You don't know how
it works then, do you?
You don't know what
sits on both sides of the scale,
what it means to decide:
what I got and what I gave,
gave that baby I didn't have,
baby who couldn't make me laugh –
applesauce upside down on her head;
couldn't make me cry –
taking his first step right off the porch.
You don't even know that this is not about regret.
You don't know one blessèd, I say *blessèd*, thing about it.

Multigravida

Three of my eggs hatched out. Just like me
and my brothers, they were all different.
One broke, I woke to find it bleeding
out of me; one I raked out early
living years on a yard with no sun;
and one came out my boy, who calls
me up from cities in the nighttime,
singing his life story through the cord.

Sleeping like a Baby

The first time the baby slept through the night
we woke up and thought he was dead.
We woke to the sun in the window:
a luxury, old wealth we had forgotten.
Then we remembered there was a baby.
We stopped breathing in the silence.
We ran to the cradle where he was
still sleeping, tiny body hot, still.
Heartbeats of heated air puffed
small from his almost wet red lips.
His little mouth was round, open
the size of a bright new nickel in sunlight.

Loverchild

a loverchild roots deep in the earth of the mother
smelling the hidden shrine, and the offering
the mother is a mountain, she is a rock
she is the cave in the rock, and she
takes the plunging fingers, she takes the groping hands
she opens to the mouth, and the tongue pushing inside
pushing up inside to the ark, to the altar
let me in mother
I'm coming in mother
please mother, please

the loverchild presses deeper and the mother groans wider
she broadens, she goes liquid
she runs with saliva, with sweat, dripping milk
her lips are swollen with blood
and the blood is purple, dark
and red, dark
rising dark like the mountain rock of the mother
like the pyramids of her nipples gripped in the fists of the loverchild
bitten by the teeth of the loverchild
mother, I'm so hungry, feed me
I need to eat you mother
I love to eat you mother
I eat to love you mother

Sometimes

Sometimes the mother says
If you kids don't be quiet
you'll be sorry;
now, I mean it.
After a while
they are quiet
and they are sorry.

Sometimes the mother says
If that baby doesn't stop crying
I don't know what I'll do.
And she doesn't
she really doesn't
even afterwards
when what she doesn't know
is what she's done.

Sometimes the mother says
If I don't get some sleep soon
I'll go crazy.
Soon comes
and soon goes
but there's no more sleep
than there ever was
so she does
she does go crazy
and she doesn't come back.

Sometimes the mother says
If I don't get some help around here
I swear to god almighty
one day

I'll walk right out that door.
There keeps on being
no help around there
so one day she walks
uptown to the bus station
buys a ticket to the farthest place
grocery money will go.
It's Springfield
where the children find her
when they get old enough
to go looking on their own
(something their father said
nobody'd ever catch him doing
and nobody ever did).

Snow, Fall

That one time you hit the baby, that one time
out on the street when the bus was so late
and then didn't come and the snow
started falling; that time you lifted all
your food in bags, paper handles dampening
and she kept holding onto your leg, pulling
your coat and you couldn't carry her too
while the flakes came thick and wet and faster.
That's the time you remember, not all
the times you didn't, all those times when
you didn't hit the baby, times you both giggled
rolled in the grass naked of anger and fear
while the teddy bear and plastic chicken
slept on top of the rackety wooden dog
without fighting. Their toy allegory is nothing
compared to that one time you saw her small face
inside the wool scarf, her wide open eyes surprised
at the slap under the hat with knitted ear flaps;
you remember that time, sharp points on every flake, falling.

Chickens

My friend Sue Ann keeps chickens, four of them
out there scratching and mumbling *bawk bawk*
right in her city backyard – the zoning laws allow this.
So do her neighbors; we're eating fresh eggs, she gives
them to us warm; bits of straw stuck to the shells,
they're dollhouse eggs, small, delicate, safe
in warm round nests shaped by hen's breasts;
not like the date-stamped cartons at the store,
their eggs trucked cold from farms outside of town.

Each hen lays an egg a day, far as we can tell:
when she finds eggs, Sue Ann takes them
right away; otherwise the hens might eat them,
not giving us a chance to scramble, boil, poach
or turn them up to their sunniest side; hens will eat
their babies raw, pecked open and picked out.
Yes, chickens eat their babies often, chicken raising
books explain; the *Cannibalism* chapters
are a big surprise. Hens seem so motherly,
their reputation domestic as an apron. Why
should they be different from the rest of us?
Should chickens be better than the rest of us
good mothers: faithful, patient, warm all day long,
waiting 'til the eggs don't need them anymore?

We know these things

On the table of time, the Mother chooses:

She knows some children cannot grow
some children will not thrive ·
will not thrive, will not, not

She sucks their breath into her lungs
holds tiny hearts between her hands
to stop their throbbing

She makes many babies, she loves many babies
some she keeps, some she keeps inside her
some she leaves, leaves them at the edge
some she kills, kills them on her altar

She feeds some from her breasts, from her mind
these ones grow strong, strong as her thighs
while some die new, small, drowning down
drowning down, down in her dark water

Information rarely offered

Maternal Instinct

Mr. Lund drove the school bus, talking
long jump, high jump, javelins; then
he wrote on the board in Science class
two reasons for the human skeleton;
we wrote them down, they were on the test,
I remember: to hold the body together,
to protect the delicate internal organs.
About the delicate internal organs
Mr. Lund explained some more:
all these eggs were in me from the start.
He didn't mention me directly, but I knew
he was saying it about me, Joan,
Beverly and Melissa too, all of us
knew what he meant, mostly.
And after that, I felt bad about it.
At twelve, I was not a good mother.
I hardly ever thought of them, and if I did,
I resented them, having to take care of them
every month, having to clean up after them,
being careful all the time because of them
(not to play with Frank and Ned at recess).
They made me tired with their mess,
embarrassed me around my friends;
sometimes, they hurt me.

Carhop, 1956: Her First Job

rock boys were in all the cars
but none of them could see
my diamond, summer red
smeared with rust from fenders

they were looking, talking
they wanted to feel
they laughed and smoked
and so did I, in back

tiny screams were in the music
I stared just like a storm
my own eyes were thunderheads
out in the gravel parking lot

all the music ran inside us
in the cars, across the trays
big cups full of shiny ice
red straws sticking up

I wrote one song myself
blaze red angel baby
bleed purple magic mother
but it was still too soon

that came later, in years
we learned to fly
in frantic blue time
dancing fire, crazy rain

Birth Control

Long ago and more recently than we think,
far away and much closer than we imagine,
women have used cervical plugs of beeswax.

They did not read this in a contraception handbook.

Some insist, despite the evidence, that drinking cold water
right before sex will make sperm sluggish; others think chicken broth
with pepper seeds will work if it burns your lips.

Women douche with rosemary, coriander, crushed willow leaves
in vinegar, powdered myrrh mixed with cloves and dried parsley tea;
these are fragrant, near-biblical, and useless.

Salt, honey and mint have never worked, but often they are
all there is, pasted up inside. The salt may burn.
Cabbage seeds won't do serious damage.

But there always have been women so desperate
they put the piss of goats and horses in their bodies, despite disgust.
Some go all the way to death: lead powder, ergot.

This has been for sex, sometimes for pleasure.

There's never been something you could be sure of, nothing
you could be sure wouldn't hurt; there always was a chance,
the gamble sometimes good, the odds sometimes bad.

Right now they're making something new. They'll say
it's safe, they'll say it's sure; they'll say anything – we know that.
But then we find, oh look, we find just eighty-seven percent.

They'll say you didn't use it right: you forgot, you waited too long,
you did it too soon; they'll say ninety-eight percent
as if it were a hundred. But two percent of us will know.

Two percent will be the data, information
rarely offered in the little paper inserts, print so small
that even if you can read, you can't read it.

She couldn't be sure what he'd say

1.

I never use condoms, you want me to feel it, don't you?
See, here's what I'll do, when I think I'm ready to blow,
I'll slide right out like a brass trombone; we won't miss a thing,
not one little thing, honey girl, you'll see. We'll both feel good,
no trouble in mind. I'm gonna protect you, honeybaby.
or
Don't you say one word, not one word; don't you make one sound,
not even the smallest sound, and don't you try to move neither, don't
you move a muscle. I don't have to tell you what'll happen
if you talk about this, do I? I didn't think so. I always knew you
were a smart girl. You always were a real smart girl.

2.

Now you know that's my baby too,
that's my baby as much as yours;
that's my son you got in there.
I know I put my boy up there;
man, I could just feel it.
or
You say it's mine but how do I know?
You're doing it with me, why not
somebody else? Other guys,
maybe lotsa guys, girl like you,
acting like you know what to do.

3.

You think I don't know what you're doing,
but let me tell you this, missy: you come in here
one day, you got yourself a big belly, you'll find
yourself out on the street, right out on the street;
now that's a promise.
or

Sweetheart, it would just kill your mother
if you got yourself in trouble, if you had
to quit school, if you couldn't graduate
with your class, if you couldn't go straight
on to college; you know that, don't you? Don't you?

Lola Dee, Cleveland Street

I heard Lola Dee never leaves the house,
not even for the paper at her door;
in the building they say,
you won't see her out here, no way

she won't answer if you knock on the door,
won't come to the window
if you ring from the street;
I know that's true, 'cause I tried it

but there was one time
she came down the back steps
to our porch, asked for cigarettes;
there she was, just like that, no introduction

she showed up in the middle of the day
when the daycare babies were out
inside the little fence we built
to keep them clear of the stairs

she came down those stairs,
leaned over the little fence,
said, got any cigarettes here?
anybody here still smokin'?

I'd never seen her before
though I'd been here two years and heard
people say she was there, up the stairs
always, up there with the kids

her eyes were big and kind of jumpy
as she leaned in over the babies;
they crawled to the fence to stare at her;
she was news to them too

we didn't smoke anymore
and the babies hadn't started;
we were a disappointment;
she came down two floors, but we were useless

she turned around, looked further down;
the last flight of stairs went right to the alley;
she stood and looked for a while;
the babies got bored, came away from the fence

I was standing close and saw her eyes
move down those steps, out the alley,
cross the street to the little store
where George had cigarettes behind the counter

she turned to my face with her eyes,
stayed one second there,
then walked back up the stairs
to the fourth floor apartment

I think about her when the babies
make a rush to the fence
or a smoker walks out to light up,
glancing 'cross the street to George's place

but I don't say, oh yes she does,
when neighbors talk about how
Lola Dee never goes out –
you know what I mean; I just don't

Movie notes *(incl. actors)*

February 7, a Sunday; open inside apartment [Clare Danes]:
She wakes slowly, eyelids slit against the light, legs
tangled into his. Sticky thighs, dry mouth. She peels
herself off the hair of his legs, skin on his knees.
He groans, mumbles, rolls over. She pulls
the pillow out from under her head, lies flat.
The condom, inside of her, leaks out onto the sheet.
She thinks aloud in short sentences: I'm pregnant.
I'm exactly pregnant. I know it. This is happening.

Cut to Marcia Gay Harden lying on sofa exhausted, wearing rumpled housecoat. James Woods' voice calls her, peremptorily. She hears, turns head, reveals bruises on face.

Back to Danes, slowly blending her face, posture, gesture with Harden:
She goes to the bathroom, comes back, lies down,
turns on her side, looks at him. She thinks aloud:
We made a baby, this man and I. We drank good
red wine, locked ourselves together wet and hot.
We made a baby. She thinks aloud, It'll look like me:
brown eyes, black curls. A girl. I'll name her
for my mother, Lenore. She imagines a ruddy baby,
made of good red wine and her mother's name.

Cut to Queen Latifah in tailored suit, juggling briefcase & papers while arguing on cellphone with her mother [Diahnn Carroll]; she gestures/whispers "Wait a minute" to a bailiff who's waving her into the courtroom.

Back to Danes, synchronizing mouth / words with QueenL:
She thinks out loud: Wait. Wait a minute. Who is this
man, really? Cute funny smart, but is he someone
to make a person with, someone to make a baby?
Wait. Wait. What about my job? And school!
I don't have money for a baby. There's no money
for this baby. There's no daddy for this baby.
I'm no mommy for this baby. She thinks aloud,
Where do I go with this? I gotta call Joanie.

Onscreen image / no sound: She calls Joanie [Sandra Oh]. They talk. She cries; Joanie cries. They both nod yes, their mouths can be seen to say yes, blending into QueenL, saying yes, nodding to judge in courtroom.

March 23, a Tuesday; on the street [open on Danes&Oh; long and wide]:
On the sidewalk, people with posters walk in a line.
They bump her and Joanie. They show them pictures,
hold up crosses. Joanie says, What's the matter with you
people? What the hell is wrong with you? Inside,
they find papers in their coat pockets. She reads hers:
Don't Kill Your Baby. She starts to cry, says to Joanie:
What are they saying? These people don't even know me.
They think I'm bad, but they want me to have a baby.

Cut to antis praying, chanting, hissing at women and girls entering clinic. Martin Sheen thrusts two small crosses, one in each hand, at Mercedes Ruehl and Jennifer Lopez; Ruehl stiff-arms him, shelters JLo with her other arm.

Back to Danes at clinic window, standing with Oh, arms linked:
She says to Joanie: Maybe they think that giving a baby
to strangers is a good idea. I guess they think that being alive
is all that matters, like breathing in and out is living.
Look at them, Joanie! Look what they're doing, scaring
that one little girl, see her? She's their own little girl.
You can see how scared she is, but they're screaming
right over her head. Well, you know what? I'm the mama
this time, not them; I'm the one deciding what to do.

Begin slow back & forth among stories of women/girls deciding whether and how to raise a child; some are essentially snapshots, echoing the stars' stories. Cast = "cross-section," like WWII platoon ensemble (waiting room = foxhole?).

Courage under Fire

Cowboys in space, Flash Gordon and the forties rocketeers
in nubby longjohns, a batch of always-blond space cadets
wearing beige, the avuncular Captain Video soon followed
by Captain Kirk, his descendants and the Darth Vader crowd;
plus tough marines smartly unlocking secret spiral notebooks,
paging fast through Pentagon rules®s, finding guidelines
to the lit-up keyboard dashboard big board control panel,
scanning table-size maps, complex charts of the ocean floor.
But mostly sailors, on battleships and submarines, sealed tight,
closed in, down inside the lightless water, nothing on the screen,
nothing outside that wide window they scan, their eyebrows
pulled together, foreheads crunched like the folds of a sandbar
until the giant lettuce waves into view, until the legendary squid
flails a tentacle, flicks one arm of suckers toward them and they see
the tattered sleeve stuck there, torn stripes just visible on that
pitiful bloody rag. The leader acts instantly, pounds the order
down, and the first mate hoarsely cries: *Abort*!

They may come back later; yes, they'll come back another day,
but now, they must think! Yes, retreat now to think! But why?
Why do they make this choice? Not because they're afraid.
We know they're not afraid. All of them are brave, except
The Skinny Guy who sweats too much, who'll die in a sudden burst
of courage, pulling someone wounded from terrifying flames.
We have seen them dive, pull off their shirts, hats, shoes and dive
into water roiling with blood, riven by huge grey fins, circling
because The Kid (underage, runaway) – who only last night
at the smoky poker game admitted he couldn't swim – fell overboard.
We have seen what happened when The Scientist – the one nobody
trusted 'til he gave a thick syringe of his own blood to save
The Black Guy – got stuck in the airlock when the water poured in
the same minute the flashing red light and siren told them
they had to shoot straight to the surface. We have seen them

brace their bodies against the surging sea and scream, "Come on, Doc! There's only thirty twenty fifteen ten seconds left!"

We have seen this many times, so we know.
We know they won't abort from cowardice
or carelessness or foolishness. We understand that
whatever it is - the secret mission, the dive
to unknown depths, ambush of the Nazi tanks,
release of the nose cone, alien freighter
spookily empty of its crew - whatever it is, they're right.
It's wrong, it's a mistake; maybe it's even *a trap*!
Thing is, they know it won't work.
They better stop. We trust them
to know it would be foolish, dangerous, wrong
to continue. Whatever has been started they know
must now be stopped. Yes! Gallant men in uniforms
[pads sewn tightly in the shoulders] can choose
under fire, even when the countdown's in their bodies,
quickening pulses. We see them sometimes decide this:
what has begun cannot continue, cannot be completed.

Patient History

The farmer raised ducks and geese, goats for milk and cheese, breeding them. She told the interviewer, *May of been twenty, twentyfive times, may of been more. I just take a good strong quill sharpen it up, dip it in turpentine.* She'd squat down, reach inside, spread her fingers, hold them wide. *Didn't hurt; it was pretty quick.* She helped her goats with those fingers, pulling a birthing kid stuck sideways, groping for slick legs, the head, turning slippery bodies with those hands. She was healthy, the report said, carried six babies to term, five still living. *They grew up all strong but the one, Micky. He started out good but then he turned around. It was the asthma, kept getting worse.... Yes, right, that one time. May of been twentyfive, may of been more; I can't say how it went wrong, or why. Maybe the one quill was just bad.*

That one time she infected, spiked a high fever, went to the clinic in town. That's how we know; they wrote it up, told the whole story: all those quills, all those times, her strong children, all those years she bred her stock, fed and raised the ones she kept. He never knew what she did, never asked a question; fell on top of her pregnant, nursing, in between. *He was quick,* she said. *But it was a match. He was near as quick putting 'em in as I was taking 'em out.*

The Bible in Everyday Life

King Solomon could not imagine this woman,
sobbing, crazy, lost in shock, this kind of mother.
He never watched the six o'clock news, where
she, sullen, covered her face with her arms,
fisting fingers that look bloody on the screen.
She was the kind whose jury needs less
than an hour to agree there's no shadow,
no doubt: she certainly was the one
squeezing the baby's shoulders, shaking it
silent like Sharon, who couldn't take the crying,
or throwing it out a window like Rosie,
so ripped she didn't know what she threw
was her baby, or beating it with metal hangers
like Margaret, her own blue bruises fading,
or seeing it strangled in the cradle like Johnette,
whose boyfriend wanted all of her attention.

Solomon didn't get to that part. Sheba left
without teaching him what might be inside
a *belly like a heap of wheat set about with lilies.*
Solomon knew how to use the sword, he said.
The King was ignorant of women (no matter
that he owned so many). He thought a woman
who let a child die was not a mother; he didn't
imagine making her baby die might be the way
a mother could be good. He never met Medea
(as far as we know); she lived in a different
mythology. Perhaps his menagerie,
like his women's rooms, was a mystery
to the King: Did he realize that panthers,
monkeys, the great loving elephant cows
tried to kill their babies quickly, with a snap
or smother, before they could grow to the cage?

The King could not imagine a woman
who needed to think about doing it early,
before, not after, her mind in hard future,
all her whispering over what might come,
all her worrying over the *maybe*. Solomon
did not think of women when he was not there,
talking like they have to, weeping;
ever never shouldn't won't can't must –
pacing back and forth through quickening:
Sooner is better than later. Do not wait
until it's old enough to know. Do not wait
until the child grows so frightened that
she runs out wild to long dark streets, runs,
sleeps, on broken glass; grows so hopeless
he hangs himself in the gymnasium, apology
to the janitor taped to the bottom of his shoe.

Don’t tell me you didn’t know this

Jocasta interviewed in Hell

Well, naturally I blamed myself – blamed myself for giving up my baby – we all do, even when we say we don't. Being queen of Thebes was no compensation, though Laius insisted it would be. I don't say he made me do it, though being king he made me understand he could have. Laius was a bully anyway, and a bit dull, as many bullies are. If he thought he could confound the oracle, if he really believed he could defeat the old ones, why did I have to make that choice? Why did I have to send my child away?

Later I understood how great his fear had been. But when we argued, while we argued, I had no idea. I was so young then, still crying over my loose belly, still soaked in milk – I had set down my own power, and he was the king. He said, Send the child away; turn it out. And I did that. I did what he asked.

And so the queen of Corinth raised my son. Her servants and tutors grew him into a strong one who left home on a tide of fear, fearfilled love for his parents – love for his *parents*! But then, like an animal with instinct for its birth blood, he came back to be my suitor, my mysterious lover, the savior of my city.

You people always ask why I didn't recognize him, but have you ever seen a newborn? Or even a dear six month infant? Do you think I have the gift, the eye of the Graiae? Do you? Can you look at such children and imagine who they'll be at 18, standing in front of you? I think not. When you look down at them in their baskets, wrapped in soft cloth, rooting for the nipple under your gown, pursing their tiny budlipped mouths toward the smell of you, their eyes still fogged, still changing? How could I have *recognized* him?

Talking about Suzie, 1959

Don't you remember *any*thing? It was just a little while ago, I think it was '56, no, it must've been '57, Suzie went away right before school got out, right at the start of summer. So what was that, your second year at Bonaventure, starting then? Sure, yeah, 'cause it was the summer before my junior year. Don't you remember, it was right around the time of spring carnival, they said she was sick and she had to stay home and finish the year with a tutor from DePaul? And then they said she had to go away, so Aunt Viv and Uncle Al took her away, but remember Teddy and all the little kids stayed with us for a week and you two took them to the beach on the bus every day? Remember it was real hot, *every*body was at the lake – except me, that was the year I got my work permit, the first time I could make more than baby-sitting money, so I could only go to the lake on Sundays after church. Anyway, that was when they took her to one of those places, *homes*, in St. Louis; they keep you there until you have your baby and then they give the baby to people who can't have kids. It was like a convent there, or a jail even, I'm not kidding, places like that are so strict, the people who ran it were really mean, worse than Sister Marie-Claire – maybe even worse than Sister Thomas. I saw this movie about a girl who had to go to one, and her boyfriend tries to find her and he finally does, and he's real cute, but they won't let him in. So Mom and Dad and Aunt Viv and Uncle Al told everybody she was at a sani*tor*ium, for breathing when you get TB or something, but she wasn't, she was in St. Louis. It *is* true. She *did*. Don't tell me you didn't know this. Suzie had a baby right before school started up again. She nearly got back too late to register; remember, because she came late she had to be locker partners with some girl in her homeroom who never talked? How can you not *remember* any of this?

Sheila's deposition, 1997

Ok, look, don't give me a hard time; I'm gonna tell everything; it doesn't matter now anyway. I need a cigarette.... All right. Here goes. In my own words, like you like to say. First of all, I never thought I'd get, you know, pregnant, because I just didn't, you know, I mean it was too stupid, I mean, like who gets pregnant? I figured nobody gets pregnant, really. And it's not like we did it that many times either. And then when it happened, it took a while before I even knew, because I wasn't always bleeding at the same time every month, I wasn't some poster girl who started every twenty-eight days like they say, so I didn't even notice at first. And I didn't want to pay any attention anyway, it's so gross, I mean, the whole thing. Like blood always gets on your hands when you change and half the time it starts when you're at school and you don't even know 'til you pull down your pants in the locker room. But when I started to get fat I got freaked out; that's when I remembered I hadn't seen my period for a while. So I went on really strict diets, almost like the anorexic girls, and I worked out as many hours as I could, and that really helped, so like nobody noticed. My father never looks at me anyway, he wouldn't recognize me on the street, I swear, and my mother is not in the picture, you know? Later, when my stomach started to stick out anyway, I just wore really long sweaters and shirts, dark, mostly black. When I was naked you could really tell; I showed Jerry in the seventh month and he said, Jeez, how much bigger is it gonna get? But I had this cool idea, I went and got – really, you won't believe this, I got a *girdle*, you know, like women used to wear in old times. I got it in the old lady section of a store downtown where nobody goes, and it worked, you know, like even when I was eight months and all the way to the end, nobody noticed anything – well, nobody ever said they did, anyway. It hurt though, I mean that girdle really hurt me. And when it finally started to come out, when I felt it hurting *under* the girdle, like from the inside, I was in school, so I got Jerry and we skipped out in his car. First we just drove around, but then he took me to a motel we used for sex, and I stayed in the bathroom until it came out. He played music real loud so nobody could hear me – I mean, I wasn't like some jungle woman or anything, but I made noise. When it came out, I turned it over and we pressed the head into a pile of towels for a while. We filled the tub with water to clean up and first we just put it all in there, the rest of the stuff that came out, you know, like the afterbirth, the cord. Jerry cut the cord with a Swiss army knife – he was very together. He used to be some kind of scout – you know, they learn stuff. We watched it float for a while, and then Jerry said, Hey, I know what we can do; let's take it to a dumpster – 'cause who looks in dumpsters, right? I mean, nobody we know does that, only maybe, like, homeless people, they might look around in there, but they're not gonna care. I mean, ok, they eat from dumpsters, but they're not gonna eat a baby, right? And it'd be dead anyway, and we can like stick it in a box, or under newspapers; nobody's ever gonna see it. So, ok, we were wrong about that part, but we did a pretty good job. You can't tell me it'd be better if we got all nice and married and kept the kid, playing Mommy and Daddy. I mean, think about it.

Birth Mothers Turn to Highest Court

That baby was luckier than Moses
I didn't put it in the river
I did what was right
I shouldn't be punished for that.
What about this double jeopardy?
I was in jeopardy once
I shouldn't have to be in it again.
I followed the rules: I never told
never asked questions
why won't they do the same?
They promised; they said nobody
would ever know, but everybody
talks about it now. It's these feminists
all this talking about choice.

Well, here was mine:
I could have had a bastard
disowned by my family
cut by everybody in town
with a skinny poor child to feed;
I could have gone to that man
who slept at the back of the gas station
probably had to fuck him first
and maybe died after;
I could get on the bus to St. Louis
live with the nice ladies
sleep on a clean white sheet
wake up with a flat belly.
That was my choice.

I did not want to be a mother
and I am not one. I gave it away.
These great big grown up people
now are greedy, that's just what it is.

They already have some parents
but they want some more.
Think of all the children
who never got even one mother –
children whose mothers died!
And here come these overgrown babies
all wanting more than their share!

Noreen's phone calls, 1999

They told me everything the day I left the hospital; they spread the papers out in front of me and I signed, but I never read them. I pretty much knew what they said. They explained the rules, about how I would never see her again, how I would never know who got her. Just like when it happened, I did what I was told. See, I was never a complainer; I was the kind that even if I fell down and hurt myself, I'd get right back up and keep walking. He lived on my block, we went out a few times; he seemed ok. We went to a movie and had ice cream after, but when we cut through the alley on the way home, he pushed me up against the back of a building. I saw him a lot on the street after that but I never talked to him. And I never told what happened, even when I knew I was pregnant. I dropped out of school and moved into the Home when it started to show. We sang hymns after supper every night, played cards every afternoon; we did a lot of laundry. They advised us to give them away; there wasn't much talk about taking care of babies. They always said the babies would be better off with their new parents; their new parents would give them good homes, send them to college. Once I was out of there, I hardly ever thought about it. That's the truth. I didn't cry when I saw babies, or wonder what she looked like; it was gone from me, like she was gone from me. It was erased, wiped out of my mind for years. Then one day I saw in the newspaper about some people who were adopted searching for their birth mothers. I'd never heard the expression before – *birth mother*. I started to cry. Picture this, I'm on the train, I don't have any Kleenex or anything, and I can't stop crying. I mean, *sobbing*. I got off before my stop, I was so embarrassed. Two days later, like I was hypnotized, I picked up the phone book, found the agency that handled the adoption, and called. While I was picking out the numbers on the phone pad, my head started buzzing – literally buzzing; I could hear this buzz behind my eyes. It stopped the second they answered. The second they picked up the phone, there was a clear silence, like a sheet of window glass, clear silence hanging in my head where the buzzing had been. Then the person on the other end said *Hello. Hello?* and I started to talk. I told them if she ever came looking, I wanted to be found. I gave them my home number and address, my number and address at the gallery, my email and cell phone – I would have given driving directions, the buses and trains that stop near me, or my social security number and my blood type – but they already had that. I didn't search on my own, hire a detective like some do. I only wanted to make myself available; in case she ever wanted to know, she could find me. And what they did was, they sent her a letter, saying if she wanted to meet her birth mother, they had the information. I didn't know it could work that way, but that's what happened. After a long time (she thought about it nearly a year) she called me. And when the phone rang – I swear to god this is true – when the phone rang, I knew before I picked it up that it was her.

Great with Child

You think you did not nurse because you did not
suckle the child, because calcium never leached
out of your bones to make that miniature elbow
and blood from your own uterus will never scab
on those still-perfect knees; because your labia
did not tear a ragged edge of red flesh
around that newborn skull, its cartilage
never molded to the walls of your vagina,
you think you may be a fraud, counterfeit;
but you are no less mammal than any lowing cow.

Snuffling like a monkey you rub your pelt
thrillingly against the child's, like dolphins you
two swim inside a wide blue sliding shadow;
and like a bitch in her den, vixen in a thicket,
you lie down and open yourself utterly
when that child comes to your body,
that child softens like wax to your body,
like your own breasts between your shoulders,
the child rides there, resting like your breasts
on your belly, feeding on you, feeding there
where your breasts wrap your heart and you
wrap the child all round with your arms, large,
grown large, you are great with the child.

That Will Never Happen

All my children are adopted. Four times
I went far away to get them: tiny girls
down from the mountains of China, small
boys up from the valleys of Romania. All
my children are foreign, strangers to the blood
and bones of me. They never grew from cells
that were mine, their first homes were other
women's bodies, they all lived first inside
of other women. Because of this, despite
knowing this, I still want to see my hair
on their heads, growing. I look for the cleft
of my chin, the knobby thumb on my right hand
and my particular nose, this same nose. I want
to see that in my children, up mountains
and down valleys of my body, of my knowing.
I'm jealous. I want to say: *I couldn't wait!*
I thought it would take forever! Nine months?
It was ninety, they always laugh out loud
on the playground. *And my breasts*, they say,
my breasts were just huge; they got so big
my blouses wouldn't button! They smile,
waiting down at the bottom of the slide.
I still want that – little boys under my skin,
pressing up against my heart from inside,
little girls elbowing around my body, poking
baby heels and chins into my spine.
That will never happen. What I want
is far away, beside the point of my whole life.

The Spade

– for S.R.

Nobody wants to call a spade a spade, a pointed shovel
sharp enough to dig into the earth, dig a small hole
smaller than a baby's grave, small as a not-done baby body,
so small nobody but the mother wants to say dead; nobody
wants to say baby, nobody wants to say dead when it wasn't
done yet. Maybe people think they'll be blamed if they say
the almost-baby is dead. Maybe. But they won't be blamed; no.
Only the mother will be blamed – everyone will say *she lost it.*
When the unfinished-baby is dead, no one will say
it's dead. Instead, they'll talk as if she left it on the bus,
dropped it in the park, stayed in the woods too long
when it got dark; she turned the wrong way off the highway,
didn't ask directions, didn't take a map. She had it with her
when she went to sleep, but waking on the white bed,
looking up at blue fluorescent tubes, she knew she'd lost it.
Some people won't blame her. The people who won't blame her
won't say she lost it; those people will say *she had a miss*. Their
different diction will not blame her, but they won't say dead baby
either. They won't say the almost-baby is dead, but they won't blame
her. There's no blame in a miss, they say; these things just happen.
Anybody can miss, or be missed, or have a miss. Like if you
oversleep, and even though you rush, you miss the train. Or if
somebody close to you, somebody very close, goes away suddenly
forever, you miss that somebody. That's how they say it then.

Abort/Retry/Fail

– for Geri

IVF and the computer, they came in together
so when the nurse pulls out your chart, that bloody record
reads just like the science on your screen

the messages they give you at the clinic
remind you of the ones you get at home
everywhere you are a woman *searching for lost chains*

sometimes the doctors tell you they are
analyzing lost clusters, like notes that flash
across your screen; they're *analyzing structures*

they promise every time that you can
close all programs, log on as a different user
but so far it hasn't worked; so far all you've done

is donate stem cells and embryos that didn't make it
inside of you, the *motherboard*; they tell you
they are hopeful, but they always *hide details*

like a junkie, a diabetic, you have your own syringe
like an opium smoker in a misty crib, you take what they give
knowing the drugs they push are dangerous

bad for you but you have to trust them, need to
trust them (mechanics using tools, knowing
a language you don't), trust them while you fear *user error*

on the Net, *scanning files,* you catch more than you can
at the clinic; fresh and frozen human
embryos, you say it's like a menu: most fish frozen so

the waiter recommends the special, which is fresh;
oh! how can you think in jokes? *scanning memory*
you find (again) laughing sometimes has to be the way

when it's all about life, all about death, all about
scanning master boot records, looking for responses
at the cellular level, *scanning boot records* for signs of life

The train is in the station

Genetic engineers are racing down the track, blowing their whistles
at all the crossings. Driving high speed trains, they're making
up for lost time. They're wearing overalls and striped caps, red
bandannas flap at their collars; it's a nostalgia trip. Every station
they pull into has a crowd on the platform, lawyers waving papers,
legislators hustling baggage. There's a lot of baggage: stem cells,
embryos, fetal tissue, *in vitro,* cloning – right off the six o'clock news.
The science guys are arguing about ethics, senators and governors
are with them, against them, paying attention to marketing, paying
consultants to pay attention to the consequences of distribution
agreements, global concerns in relation to local issues, business
interests and the Fed. Hit your remote to see philosophers, sociologists
get their licks in; they profess in sound bites, answer Jay and Dave
with a smile but take Ted seriously. Doctors want to get right
in the game, want to use their own patients, take meetings
with drug company reps – they're the major players of course, big
piece of action there. Everybody's paying attention now. Some people
in the parking lot look like they're in costume – it's the religious
leaders in their gowns and funny hats. They were chanting but
now they see the Pentagon's here, they've stopped; instead
they're forming coalitions across doctrinal lines. Everybody knows
that in the funding leagues, genes and cells each won their pennant,
so now it's the world series of proposals, federal money edging up
pharmaceutical money, money from foundations with agendas. Genes
are favored by all the bookies, and this train is carrying gamblers,
some crap shooters and midnight ramblers in addition to consultants
from elite research universities; some say Harvard trumps Stanford
trumps Columbia, but what about MIT and Chicago? The brokers
have a private car; the Internet people are on a wait-and-see basis.
The corporations want to get ad campaigns started, want to know
when the logos click in, want to set up the media outlet connections.
They know this could get sticky, could take a lot of time (it's babies,
feelings, families) but they're confident; their track record is solid.

All these

Let us assume it has been decided: it is good
to set aside the woman, avoid use of the human
whenever possible. Let us assume technicians

have devised a formula: salt and water
flow into a basin of recent devising,
duplicate the great maternal wash, pre-history,

even a beach we can crawl out onto,
amphibious for that fraction of a moment,
briefly bleary-eyed, and chilled. Nevertheless

there is a challenge. What must be done,
what's needed, is re-creation of the mother shell
surrounding, touching every fetal cell of us.

Because not only a mother's heart
(that over-written metronome of metaphoric
rhythm rocking the cradle of every little nucleus)

but also the yoga of her lungs, sucking oxygen
down into the tiniest intricate branches,
squeezing carbon dioxide

from those shining pink trees; also struggle
of intestines pushing oatmeal,
green beans, lamb chops, chocolate cake

through their bumpy tunnel,
tightening urethra and rectum
for the rush of urine, thrust of thick feces;

also momentum of sex, when mama tightens,
growls, heaves, and moans so low
that only the baby, the baby can hear her

coming, pulsing tidally into orgasm, shuddering
amnionic fluid, fetal flesh, soft bone of fontanel –
all these insist small bodies absorb pleasure bonded

to amino acids, tactile destiny in trace minerals.
If accuracy is the goal of our gestation engineers,
all these are factors in the problem solved by birth

environment theory. To render the virtual, consider
the actual: membranes aroused by what's beyond
the womb, perhaps beyond control or duplication.

Women

can move like birds,
rising quickly, landing surely

we rise suddenly, moved to flight,
then swooping, land again
in what seems the same place

we rise as one bird,
from a branch mid-high

we go far off, so far
the mark on the sky disappears.

For all the Mary Catholics

Mary Catherine came to public school because of money,
sat down next to me; Mary Elizabeth stood behind us
on the line in gym, whispering I ought to join
the Brownies; Mary Frances shared a geography book
(there never were enough in Miss King's room);
sweet Mary Jean showed me a shortcut home,
dangerous, down the alley (now she drives high
school girls across state lines, skipping
parental consent); Maria Teresa showed me
newborn puppies in a basket, then cut me cold
when I would not sing Jesus in December;
cute Mary Alice had a crush on my brother,
sighing they never could marry; famous Mary Jane
with her shiny black shoes traded me St. Francis
for a gas station pinup; Mary Rose shared
my locker, my Kotex, my Kleenex; Mary Ellen kissed
me on the mouth and laughed; shy Mary Jo
worshipped Audrey Hepburn in the dark; quiet
Mary Ann died at the Shut-Eye Motel,
blood from her uterus crusted on her thighs; tough
Mary Margaret moved to Detroit, seven children,
eight years, never answered letters; funny
Mary Louise called her Dungannon brogue
a French accent; Maria Francesca prays outside
the clinic where I work; Mary Patricia (now M. Pat)
called me after thirteen years to ask, Is the pill
safer now? then got divorced and married my brother;
Mary Helen marched with me all the way
down State Street, holding Mary Magdalene
over our heads; and angry Mary Carol goes to Mass
for the music, the poetry, the rush of spirit,
crying in pure nostalgia: *They can't keep me out!*

Opposing Arguments

Doctors are supposed to preserve life, not end it *and* People will have no posterity if they kill their children *and* At eight weeks, it's fully developed, has fingerprints, a beating heart *and* Don't talk to me about soldiers, the electric chair, police; these are innocent babies *and* Women are supposed to be mothers, that's what women are for *and* Oh, she'll change her mind when the baby comes *and* If my mother knew I'd never walk, she'd have done it *and* There is no population problem; all the people in the world could stand inside New Jersey *and* There's enough oil in Alaska for all we'll ever need *and* Don't you bring that feminist middle class mind in here; we know abortion equals genocide *and* Lots of women would love to have the babies you people throw away *and* Filthy sluts, opening their legs; let them lie in the filthy beds they made *and* Moral disregard for the life of the fetus spreads moral insensitivity through society *and especially* Only the Lord God truly chooses; no one but God may take a life.

Obstetrician Murdered by Terrorist in Amherst, New York

The doctor went into the kitchen
where if you can't stand the heat
you don't stand by the window
and he stood there, he came in
to maybe drink a glass of water,
and there was a window in the kitchen
with no blinds, no shade, no curtains
closed in front of the doctor
while he drank his glass of water
while the man outside pulled the trigger.

In the newspaper, on television
the police chief said he thinks
that shooting was the doctor's fault
the doctor was not careful
the chief had told him not to
stand there in the kitchen
by the window, not to put butter
on bread, no strawberry jam, no soup
in front of the window
with no shades or blinds or curtains.

All the doctors who want a glass of water
were told not to stand, they were told
to pull the shades
shut the curtains
close the blinds
but maybe the doctor wanted –
maybe he wanted to live
his own life, as long as he had it –
he wanted his life to stand:
he wanted to stand in his own life.

Back and Forth

Looking for meaning, I found, first, that *roe* is
a small species of deer inhabiting parts of Europe and Asia.
But that wasn't it, so I looked further and found *the mass*
of eggs contained in the ovarian membrane of a fish;
that looked good right up to the last word: *fish.*
There was *hard roe*, a commentary until defined
as *the spawn of a female fish*, *soft roe* being *the milt*
or sperm of a male fish. Not to the point after all,
but now I was up to 1430. Persevering, I discovered *roed,*
which by 1611 had come to mean *full of spawn.*
That was certainly true, and one *wade* in the OED
was *some kind of fishing net* (1388). Despite that
surprise, that coincidence of confluence, I kept looking.
I could've gone to metaphor, scooped up roe for caviar,
but that was not useful. Surely *Beowulf*, composed
(they think) around 1000, should take pride of place.
When used to discuss persons and animals in that year,
the word meant *go, advance, move onward*, carrying
some of our own concerns; it meant *chiefly to go over*
or through something. When speaking of weapons,
wade cut straight across a thousand years *to go through,*
to penetrate into something – they'd known this in 993.
One hundred years before that they'd already begun to say
wade meant to *walk through any soft substance* impeding
motion (tall grass, deep sand, legislation, demonstration, fear).
Formerly often, they used it to mean *pass over a river on foot*
but passage, or getting over, did not remain its meaning, on foot
or otherwise. They did, however, keep the *[rarely used]* phrase
to wade (up) to the knees, armpits, etc. Current usage justifies,
sometimes amplifies, this retention of meaning. By 1374,
they said the word *wade* meant *to go* not only *in action,*
but also in *thought or discourse,* (even, simply) *to proceed.*
Unfortunately obsolete is the 1386 phrase *to wade out of,*
meaning *to escape from.* We could sure use that one.

By 1398 they might have become jaded, dwelt more
upon the meaning of law than the meaning of life, a danger
we face today, as some confuse being alive with living.
I see that by then the figurative usage of *wade* was *chiefly,*
to go through a tedious task, a long or uninteresting book.
But as in this time, many tables turned with the century:
by 1400 a new context had been born; carried to term
it implied, especially, *to wade through blood, slaughter, etc.*
In that round new year, who defined *right*, and *life*? What
did they mean? Who decided what life may be, when
it begins and whether to end it? In 1527, they must
have argued these questions as we do, using their *wade,*
meaning *to continue discussion with a person.* Much later,
in 1714, they saw there'd be no resolution; by then
they knew that *wade* meant *to persevere under difficulties.*

One lovely bit from the middle of the nineteenth century
explained that in sawn mahogany, *roe* was *that alternate*
streak or flake of light and shade running in the grain,
but I couldn't see yet how that shimmering sometime flash
would be a bright image still, through all the years of rowing
back and forth, back and forth across the widest lake.

Here, in the heart of the country

Woman Finds Truth

Ms. Debbie Pfister of Downers Grove, Illinois was staying at the RiverView Inn downstate in Rock Island when it happened.

She told our reporter: "You know how when you're sleeping in a strange place you sort of feel along the walls in the dark when you get up to go? And when you flick on the bathroom light just for a second to get your bearings, it's a blinding flash, and you see it, like on the back of your skull? Probably, maybe, like a nuclear bomb would be? Well, that's when it happened. I flicked the switch, and there it was: The Truth."

Asked if the experience had changed her life, Ms. Pfister said, "Well, some days are so ordinary you'd think it never happened, it's just regular me, you know, like I've always been. But some days, Wow!"

Facts of Life

– for Ruella

You don't have to stand in the street, six-guns
glinting high noon sun; you don't have to be
American, sixteen and angry at the teacher.
All that we do, living, is killing; birth
and death the pumping hearts of life.
What's born is born from death. Every cell
inside us, every cell that makes us; skin
of our faces, facing each other with cells
falling away, cells rising: lips, eyelashes,
cheekbones dying, being born.

Beyond these facts of life, involuntary
cellular facts, what counts is the voluntary
thinking creature living beyond fact,
inside metamorphosis. Crucial in moments
of transition (all moments being
moments of transition) is that inside
the taking and giving, you are conscious.
You are responsible. You know.
So when you decide to open the bottle,
count pills out with your fingers, turn
up the morphine with your thumb,
switch the electric current off – or on,
push the plunger of the syringe,
shoot straight fast into the body
of someone you don't know, release
the catch of the bomb bay, cut down
the field of ripened rye, pull off
all the berries, pluck the reddest apples,
cut the throat of the biggest ram
or the smallest lamb, close the eyes
of the very old dog, the senile cat
who slept years in the curve of your back,
you know. You know everything.

Hard times, fast river

Don't you just hate it when you start to cry
and other people think you're crying
because of something they know
but you're not
you're not
you're crying because
what's happening
has knocked the heart of your memory sideways
and the pain, the pain
of that sideways heart
is making you sob
sobs struggle out around the pushed in part of your lungs
where the heart is pressing
and your throat is too thin
the sobs fill it up
you can't breathe
you can't stop crying
and the people keep hugging you
touching you
saying they understand
when they don't
they don't
they don't even know
they don't.

Being Alive

I never said I killed my baby, never said it like you do,
like it was a bad thing to do, a bad thing for the baby.
You think being alive is everything, you think
being alive is all that matters, you say life is Sacred,
whatever that means, that what starts must not be stopped
except by God, whatever that means; you believe
that all those cells, dividing, are necessary, necessarily
good. You can't imagine this multiplication of division
as cancer, this growth as malignant, for its own life,
its own whole breathing life, pulled out into your world.

In the Service we said

In the Service we spoke clearly and distinctly:
We said, This is Jane from Women's Liberation;
please leave your name, your number and a message.
We'll call you back. When she did, we did; then
we said, What was the date of your last period?

When we met to talk, we said, Are you sure
you want to do this? When she said Yes,
we said syringe, speculum, dilator, curette;
we said vagina, we said cervix, we said uterus,
telling how to open it from the outside;
sometimes we had to say forceps, placenta, labor,
trimester, hours, contractions, fetus.

(To each other, learning, we said it feels like
the roof of your mouth, those ridges up in there;
the curette scrapes along those ridges, spoonlike.
We said you can feel the shape, like a textbook
illustration; it feels just like the picture looks,
it feels just like you think it will; that helps. Later,
sometimes we said, She was more afraid of the shot
than anything else. Or we said, Her cervix was so tight,
I thought I'd be there for an hour, my arm frozen,
my shoulder numb, holding that dilator still.)

Lying there, some would ask, so we said No,
we're not doctors; we're women just like you.
We needed to know how, so we learned it –
you know, just like you learn anything.

The Abortion Counseling Service of the Chicago Women's Liberation Union, now called "Jane" in histories of women's health movement in the USA, worked with more than eleven thousand women and girls (the youngest under twelve, the oldest over fifty), all of whom came to the underground group for abortions before the Supreme Court decision on Roe v. Wade in late January of 1973. Women in the group always called it "the Service," and referred to ourselves as "Janes."

City Living, Chicago

Living in the city is like living
in the shell you put up to your ear
the roar is distant, constant
and it's not the ocean.
Here the roar in your ears is
like the night in your eyes
mercury orange sky surrounding you
like the shell surrounds your ear.

Living in the city, the lake is not the ocean
but when you stand at the harbor fence
you maybe think it is
because that edge, the end of the world
looks just as forever here, in Chicago
as it does in Bermuda
a flat sheet of blue to horizon or green like a waterbird's belly
or gray waves tearing the line that separates air and water.

And the gulls are shrieking from Indiana
walking concrete piers in Michigan
flying over the chess pavilion
here in Illinois. This could be Atlantic City
it could be the ocean
if you didn't know about Wisconsin
if you didn't know this water is surrounded
but living in the city, you do.

Applied History

This really happened. I read it in the papers.
The Reverend John Earl, one year younger than Jesus
at the end, pastor at St. Patrick's in Rochelle, Illinois,
thirty miles south of Rockford, young Father John
(as parishioners must have called him) drove his car
up into Rockford. Then he rammed it
into an abortion clinic at eight-fifteen in the morning
the last day of September, year 2000.
Then he got out and chopped at the building
with an ax. Then Father John was arrested,
charged with *burglary, felony criminal*
damage. Reports said *damage was confined*
[exterior overhead door, woodwork in a hallway].
How is damage *confined*? How does that work?
The priest was released, the papers said: ten thousand
dollars *bond*. Is it the *bond*, then, that does the confining?
The probably small diocese of Rockford (not grand
like Chicago, no brick mansion on the park) issued
a written statement: Father John's *activities* were *restricted*
while the matter is reviewed. What would that be,
do you think? The review, I mean. What would be
viewed again? We need to ask because
that statement, historically framed, was lacking
the Inquisition, Crusades, and holy wars
of public and private record, declaring simply that
it has never been nor is it...policy or practice
of the Roman Catholic Church to condone, approve
or promote violence...to achieve a desired end.

Women's Liberation

– for Esther

Every week we went to a meeting,
but not like now. No one stood up
and said, My name is Jane and I'm
an abortionist. No. Because we didn't
want to stop, we weren't trying not to do it.
We sat in apartments, passing the cards.

One card is Sandy from West Lafayette,
eighteen years old, coming in on the bus.
She's got about sixty-three dollars, she thinks
she's nine weeks pregnant. The next card is
Terrelle, who's thirty-two and angry. Her
doctor gave her an IUD that didn't work;
he says there's nothing he can do.
Here's Mona, fifty-four years old, has one
hundred dollars, wants to keep this secret
from her family. And Carlie, a long term –
twenty weeks pregnant, may have ten dollars,
twelve years old like Mona's youngest – she
got herpes from her brother when he did it.

Every week some of the cards were passed
around for hours; none of us wanted
to counsel those women, take one
into her life. The longest of long terms,
they lived far away, had no one but us,
no one to tell, no one to help, no money.
They needed everything. Cards went around
the room while we talked: dilation, syringes,
xylocaine, the Saturday list. At the end
of the meeting, all the cards were taken.

The Teacher at Home, 1970

One night as I was eating complementary proteins for my health
the phone rang and the young voice said she'd just come back from
    Boston
had I ever been there? *Yes* (and, I thought, Berkeley and Boulder too).
And that Boston was so exciting, I mean, all kinds of action and
coalition and collectives and everything, so much more political
than Chicago, she said. I thought: Well! I mean, jeez,
could anything be more political than Chicago?
But, realizing I'd take us nowhere useful that way
in this short conversation I mean, I said *mmm mmm mmm*
at helpful, interested intervals to my sweet student
(an energetic youth, she orders burgers with everything)
and then I went back to a dinner designed to keep me thinking.

I went back to blue-green broccoli, organic
to save my life here in Chicago, with speckled beans
and shining red pepper that bleeds when you cut it
and rice that's brown, like the dirt at the farm in the zoo.
I thought of the cows above Boston, the black and white cows of
    Vermont,
their yellow cream so thick that it could turn my heart against me.
Here, in my own kitchen. Here, in the heart of the country.

Glenda Charleston, 1971

A woman came to us, seventeen
weeks, nervous. Maybe scared,
like Julie said. Her eyes were steady,
dark. But I'd seen scared,
and Glenda Charleston was different –
holding back, but not afraid to do it.

Her vulva was a wall, labia taut.
I had to massage her feet and belly,
rub her forehead. Then she relaxed,
let her thighs fall open,
let the speculum slide inside,
one smooth motion, in and open.

Then yellow pus poured out of her,
creamy pus, running thickly
down the plastic sheet: she tried it
before she found us. Maybe a hanger,
knitting needle, crochet hook. Maybe
a pencil with a sharpened point.

(She'd faked her temperature:
took the thermometer out, held it
up in cool air, waited ten, fifteen,
twenty seconds. Then Julie
came back, smiled, said *Ready*?
Glenda smiled too, said *Yes*.)

We pulled the speculum out, cleaned
her perineum, thighs, buttocks.
You have a bad infection. We can't do this.
You should go to the hospital.
Go now. Julie will drive you.
But she grabbed my arm.

No! You have to do it! I brought money!
I can't have this baby. You can't make me.
Nobody can make me. I said I was sorry.
I said *Please get dressed. We can't do this.*
She was not crying. Tears filled, then
covered up her eyes; they closed her eyes.

Here is what happened.

She was fifteen years old. She had
to pay for college. She had to pay
for this. She came to my apartment
on a Saturday afternoon. Her parents
didn't know. I didn't know her parents.
Her girlfriends brought her up
the stairs, holding on to her hands.
They wanted to help. I told them,
Go; get orange juice.

She was five months pregnant.
Two days before, we reached
up inside, pushed down outside.
She breathed out like fire,
she gushed out salty water.
She was lucky it came soon:
Saturday, no school, girlfriends
who lied for her. When she called,
contractions starting, I said, *Come over.*

She sat on the floor. She bent her knees.
She rocked and pushed and rocked
inside contractions: they were close.
We were close. I never saw her again.

Her name was Rachel. She said, *I don't
want to see it.* When I took it away,
she cried. I washed her body, fresh
water, holding her like the girlfriends.
She drank her juice. She took her medicine.
I drove her to a corner two blocks
from her house. She walked home
from there *Because*, she said, *you know.*
She touched my shoulder: *Thank you.*

Felony Booking, Women's Lockup, 11th and State: A Short Literary Epic

None of us had been in jail before: middle and working
class women with education, fresh as daffodils;
we were all students, housewives, mommies
casual potsmokers, rudimentary feminists
and here's the thing, citizens: criminal abortionists
charged with several counts (Monte Cristo,
Dracula): all felonies, nothing small.

Compounded by conspiracy: *collaborators*
like in black&white movies about Nazis
where they shave the heads of women who fuck
the enemy. But, citizens, here's the thing you need
to know: when it's illegal, abortion's homicide.
It must be different now (things get different
in thirty-three years) but then, the guard held your hand.

She wasn't rough but she was tough, that Dawn:
she left us rosy-fingered, first left, then right, each
finger and thumb in a labeled box on special paper;
rolling the tips, steady for clear prints, she put
each one down in place, rocked it side to side
like shaping dumplings: pierogi, ravioli.
Both hands done, she picked up a flat wooden stick.

I thought: oh, she's going to put it on my tongue,
look down my throat – but she dipped it into a jar
of yellow-white slime, dropped a smear onto
my hands, looked into my eyes and said, *Clean 'em off.*
I thought it was but knew it couldn't be mayonnaise.
She gave me a grey paper towel, already turning
to the next woman, reaching for her hands.

The next guard: big woman with metalgrey hair.
She'd seen it before, knew why we were there:
seven white women in jeans and t-shirts,
mine tight over breasts aching long past time.
Our guide to the cells, she looked right in my face,
her own unmoving when she said *Come on,*
I'll put you in with your partner.

Our cell had no bars. Walls and doors were dark
metal sheets, ceiling a steel grate, heavy wood plank
along one wall, gritty sink and toilet small
as toys: Barbie's Cell. Dank wind swirled across
the floor, pooling on the grey concrete like water.
Women screamed all night: no words, only screams.
That was the third place we were taken.

The second was a cage: the holding pen. There we met
two women arrested for smashing a window, stealing
a tv set. One was tiny, all dressed up: heels, nylons, lipstick.
One was fifteen, five months pregnant, scars on her arms
she'd burned with cigarettes. Black thread stitches
embroidered the wrist she cut last week. We knew
that soon, too soon, darkness would cover her eyes.

The first place was Cottage Grove: sounds like little
houses in the greenwood (seven Gretels) if you're not
from Chicago. Handcuffed inside the wagon
locked clanking to a hook atop the broad van door,
twisting my body on the icy metal bench, arms
stretched up high, wrist welts rising red and classic
(Prisoner of Chillon, Man in the Iron Mask).

At the station, cuffed to an iron ring on the wall
of an office (chair, desk, cabinets, phone, calendar,
chains) for interrogation: I needed the bathroom.
Some of that time my memory says I was free, says we
were seven women standing, arms linked at the shoulder
(a chorus line of innocent ignorant felons smiling
for photographs): could that have happened?

I've seen mug shots: dark long wavy hair caught up
at the back of my head, work-ready. In profile I'm
pigeon-chested: Nursing Mother Arrested for Abortion
is the caption. I look like my stout old aunts, their fronts
the porches of bungalows. Mine is swollen hard with milk:
eighteen hours since I nursed the baby, sailed out across
the wine-dark sea, committed multiple felonies, got busted.

Locked up, I freed my breasts from their container:
a nursing bra built like the Golden Gate Bridge.
I squeezed them soft like a lover, milked them hard
like a farmer, sprayed my baby's own sweet nectar
down that dirty little sink. Then lawyer boys took me
out to night court in the basement, away from the women,
saying *strategy*: I was a wooden horse, a night mare.

Inside of me six more were riding; I was precedent:
low bail for madonna meant the same for all: a bet
with me the marker. Citizens, here's the thing: that judge
smiled right at me, called me Mrs., asked about my health.
Believe it: he smiled, said he'd send me right on home
to feed my little baby. He struck his own desk twice
with a wooden hammer: *Let it be written. Let it be done.*

Yes and No

yes; it's true, we killed babies, none of them born yet
none of them born yet to mothers born a tiny while ago themselves
mothers who were their babies' sisters, sharing the very same daddy
mothers with plenty of babies already, more than enough
mothers whose babies were all grown up, long grown up
mothers who got babies punched inside, shoved up hard inside
none of them born to mothers who wanted no babies at all
who wouldn't feed them, didn't need them, couldn't keep them
so those babies, none of them born yet
never rolled their eyes back in their heads when they got slapped
never had to ask who their mama was, or their daddy
nobody ever told them it was their fault she couldn't finish school
they didn't fall down a lot, go to the hospital late at night
their mama didn't live with new daddies to make the rent
they never sucked soda pop from rubber nipples on the bus
and they never had to cry in a locked apartment while their mama
said *I can help whoever's next* when it was never them; no

She Said

– before 1973

On the phone she said, I have a friend who's got a problem, but she couldn't get to a phone so I'm calling for her. Do you know what I mean? Is this the right place?

When she lay down, she said, Are you a doctor?

Then she said, Aren't you afraid you'll get caught?

When we were putting in the speculum, she said, Oh, I had breakfast before I came. I know I wasn't supposed to but I was so hungry I just ate everything in sight, is that ok?

Later she said, I think I have to throw up.

Or, I have to go to the bathroom right now. Stop. I just have to go to the bathroom, and then I'll come right back.

Or, on a different day, I don't feel so good, should I do it anyway?

The next week she said, Infection? I don't have any infection. Oh, that. That's not really an infection. That infection's nothing, I've had it before, it's nothing, go on, go ahead and take that baby out.

Sometimes she said, Can I see it before you throw it away?

But another time she said, I don't want to look at it, ok? When it comes out, I'll just close my eyes, and you take it away, ok?

Once she said, What do you do with it all at the end of the day? Boy, you people are gonna get in trouble sometime, this's against the law.

And when we were done she said, What if it happens again? You know – this. Would you do me again?

She stood on the back steps outside the counselor's apartment and said, This is mi prima, my cousin, from Mexico. Can you talk Spanish to her? ¿Habla un poco? ¿Un poquito? ¡Si, gringa! We will do this.

No, I'll keep it on, I'm not hot, it's ok, I'm fine. *She was wearing her boyfriend's baseball jacket in the kitchen. She said*, Just tell me what I have to know.

This is my husband, Ed. He's going to sit here with me. *She leaned over, touched his arm, and said*, Ed, honey, this is Julie, she's my counselor, the one that got assigned to me when we called the number.

When we told her she should pay whatever she could afford, she was quiet a minute and then said, I think I can get nine dollars.

My father brought me here today. He's paying for this but he's really mad at me for it. *She took a hundred dollar bill out of her pocket and said*, He thinks if everybody got liberated, like with civil rights, that there'd be a lot of trouble, and he says I prove his point, because look what happens when you just do what you want. He says that's why we have to have so many laws on everybody, because if you let people be free and do what they want they'll just do evil things.

When the sister-in-law was asked why she called the police, she said, It's a sin, she can't do this. She has to have it, we all have to. Jesus doesn't want her to get rid of this baby, that's why I did it.

He doesn't like me to talk to my mother. Him and his mother, they don't let me go home to visit. *She put the tiny baby in her mother's arms and said,* We sneaked to come for this appointment. He doesn't know I'm pregnant again. My baby is so new, I can't have another one right away. He wouldn't even want it really, he thinks this one makes too much noise. He doesn't like me to do anything without his permission.

Holding her purse, wearing her gloves, the girl clinging to her coat sleeve, she said, You take good care of her, she don't know no better, she's just a baby her own self, she don't even know how this happened. She don't know what it's all about, this whole thing.

My mother told me I couldn't keep it, she told me she'd get the baby taken away from me right away if I had it. *She cried, loud crying with snot and choking. She wiped her nose and said,* She knows I want to have it. I could be a good mother, I've taken care of babies and I know what to do. But I'm only fifteen so she'll get them to take it away from me, I know she will. That's why I'm doing this! I'd rather not even see it!

After the cervical injection, she said, How did you learn all this? Did you read a book? Is there a book?

Every now and then she said, How come you let us bring our boyfriends over to your house to wait? Aren't you afraid they'll tell? *And,* Jeez, who are all these little kids? What're you guys doing, running a kindergarten on the side? Are those doughnuts for us?

When we finished talking and gave her our phone numbers, she said, What if it comes out alive? What should I do then? I can't have it be alive. Should I, you know, should I...? Can I do it by myself? It could be alive, right?

Now and then she said, Oh I'm so sick, what a mess, oh I'm so sorry, I really feel fine but this just happened oh oh here it comes again. Oh god I'm so sorry, I can't help it, I'm such a mess, oh thank you.

She rang the bell, and when we buzzed her in she said, My girlfriends are downstairs. They brought me over when I called you about the cramps. Should they come back for me or can you give me a ride home? How long will it take for it to, you know, all come out?

Another time, waiting to miscarry, she said, I'm sorry it's taking so long. I'm sure you've got other things to do, I know a lot of women are waiting. But thank you so much, thank you for letting me come to your house. I couldn't have done this at my house, for sure. My parents think I'm at my girlfriend's house, I just hope they don't call to check on me, 'cause my girlfriend's mother could say something wrong and then I'd really be in trouble.

Ok, it'll take me about an hour and a half to drive home – I live over the line in Indiana - and here's what I'm going to do, *she said one winter weekend*. My father's a heavy sleeper, so if the cramps come in the night while he's sleeping he'll never hear me; I'll just go in the bathroom and lock the door. I'll do it all in there. He won't even hear the toilet flush, he never does, even when it's just ordinary, you know, flushing for regular reasons.

She looked at the clear plastic sheet on the mattress, the speculum and the syringe. Then she laughed and said, You ladies somethin, doin this up in here; you somethin, all right.

Why do you do this? *She looked around the small bedroom and said*, You're not rich. With what you charge, you can't be doing this for the money. What's it all about? Are you a bunch of women's libbers? Is that it?

I'm not nervous. I think you are good women. I'm never nervous, maybe cuz I'm always tired. *She was so tired that when the woman beside the bed rocked her shoulder softly to wake her up, she said,* It's over? I'm sorry, I just closed my eyes after the shot you gave me down there. I'm sorry, but I was real tired, I had to work a double shift and din have no time between work and here.

Ohmygod, does this happen all the time? This bleeding? *She gasped and said,* The blood is so dark. Ooh! Ice?! Ay! Make it stop! This ice tray is too cold! Ohmygod! You better not be scared, I'm the one scared, not you. Orange juice, are you kidding? Ay, what if I faint? I know people faint when they lose blood. Can you still do me? Did you finish?

She leaned over to the woman driving and quietly said, My daughter's in Children's Memorial, she's only two, she's having an operation on her stomach valve today – it doesn't work right, since she was born. My husband's over there, with her, for that, while I'm here, for this. Could I leave right after I'm done? Could you take me back right away, so I don't wait 'til everybody is done? Would that be ok? Would the other women mind, do you think?

She gulped some water in the kitchen and said, Oh thank you, you'll never know what this means to me. Thank you so much. I could never thank you enough, I'm sure. I know some people say it's wrong, abortion, that you shouldn't take a life. And maybe we did take a life. But it's all give and take, isn't it? My mother always said that everything comes down to give and take. So I think the baby, today, that was the taking – and me, me in my own life, I think that was the giving.

Notes

Except where noted, the names of characters (and some locations, including a high school, a motel, etc.) in all poems and monologues are fictitious; I made them up.

"Patient History" is inspired by my memory of reading, at the age of seventeen, a pamphlet I believe was published by the Alan Guttmacher Institute (or its forerunner). That text told stories like this one, about the desperation, courage and wit of women.

"Jocasta interviewed in Hell" is based on the Greek myth. Readers wanting to learn about Jocasta, Laius, their son Oedipus, Corinth, Thebes and the Graiae can find them in the classic source in English, Edith Hamilton's *Mythology,* and many other books.

"*Abort/Retry/Fail*" contains computer jargon (in italics) – mostly error messages, as well as IVF, an abbreviation for *in vitro fertilization.*

"Applied History" includes names of actual places and an actual person as well as quoted language (in italics) drawn directly from newspaper accounts of the event; these accounts may be found in libraries and on the Net.

"In the Service We Said," "Women's Liberation," "Glenda Charleston, 1971," "Here is what happened.," "Yes and No" and "She Said" are drawn from my experience in the Abortion Counseling Service of the Chicago Women's Liberation Union. The Service is called "Jane" in texts and discussions of the history of women's health; the women who were members of the Service are generally called Janes. I was a Jane for two years (1970-72). Readers interested in learning about the Service should visit *cwluherstory.org,* view the documentary film by Nell Lundy and Kate Kirtz, "Jane, An Abortion Service" (1995, Juicy Productions, PO Box 411574, San Francisco, CA 94141); and read *The Story of Jane* by Laura Kaplan (Pantheon, 1995).

"Felony Booking, Women's Lockup, Eleventh and State: A Short Literary Epic," like its literary precursor, Homer's *Iliad*, treats an actual event: the arrest, in early May of 1972, of seven members of the Service. The poem includes the actual name/location of the women's lockup in Chicago in 1972 (now changed/moved with the jail) and one actual neighborhood precinct (Cottage Grove). I chose a name for the guard with only Homeric concerns in mind.

About the Author

Judith Arcana was a Jane, a member of the Abortion Counseling Service of the Chicago Women's Liberation Union, for two years. Her poems, stories, essays and articles appear in many journals and anthologies. Her other books are *Our Mothers' Daughters, Every Mother's Son,* and *Grace Paley's Life Stories, A Literary Biography.* A native of the Great Lakes region, she lives now in Portland, Oregon.

Order Form

Chicory Blue Press, Inc.
795 East Street North
Goshen, CT 06756
860/491-2271
860/491-8619 (fax)
sondraz@optonline.net
www.chicorybluepress.com

Please send me the following books:

_____ copies of *What if your mother* at $15.00

_____ copies of *The* Love *Word* at $18.00

_____ copies of *Resistance* at $16.00

_____ copies of *Family Reunion* at $18.00

_____ copies of *The Crimson Edge* at $17.95

_____ copies of *A Wider Giving* at $14.95

Name ____

Address ____

____

Connecticut residents: Please add sales tax.

Shipping: Add $3.50 for the first book and $1.50 for each additional book.